Postscripts of a Marionette

Postscripts of a Marionette

A-NUMBER IN THE SYSTEM

———————

ISABEL VALENCIA

ALEgRÍA
PUBLISHING

From the rough times and little glimpses of light, to the happiness we share in each and every moment we spend together, I would simply not be who I am without any of you... my family.

To my fellow immigrants who find themselves struggling through the immigration system, don't lose faith for unbeknownst to us, even when the light starts to flicker, hope will guide us through our hurdles.

INTRODUCTION

My life is far from a dream come true. It is a path that I believed for many years I had chosen to take. I have come to the realization that most of the choices I made were part of the control the immigration system had on my life.

I was seven years old when my parents had to make a choice for their seven children and decided to cross the San Ysidro border to the United States. In 1986, in pursuit of a better life, they decided to strive for that "American Dream." Perhaps that was the beginning of my current path, but I'm yet to find out.

Most of my life, I felt as if someone else was pulling my strings-either the system or an entity that controlled my choices-and I never understood why. I do not expect people to understand or place themselves in my shoes. Hell, I find myself questioning if my footsteps were ever even my own.

I started this writing process as a way to discover my purpose and found that I have so much more to dig into before I can find out what that purpose is. Writing anecdotes about my life is my way of trying to decipher certain periods of my life and how they relate to my poetry. What I have uncovered so far is just a hint of a life that makes little to no sense in my unfinished story.

I hope you're not looking for a blissful ending. I'm just living life day by day as carefree as I can, and what it brings might not be my choosing by design. However, what I do know is that my family is the one rewarding choice I will continue to make every single day of my life.

TABLE OF CONTENTS

| SUEÑOS |

"Run! Run! Run!"

I was only seven years old, but I heard these words, and I did not understand what was happening around me. The confusion embraced me with a chill of tremors that fog my memories. Just a few minutes before, I was crying from the pain in my legs, when suddenly, a hand covered my mouth. Then, we were running through the hills, and I kept hearing, "Run, run, run! Hurry! Run faster!"

Eventually, it seemed like we had gotten away from danger and although we were all exhausted, we had to keep going or we would be caught.

We had finally stopped running since it appeared we had outrun the danger of being chased. After a moment, we then found ourselves walking at a pace that enabled the clouds surrounding my memories to dissipate and gave me time to look back at what had just happened.

Looking through the haze I remembered what brought us to this moment. A few months earlier, my parents made the decision to migrate the rest of the family to the United States and join my father and brother. So, my mother, three older sisters, two brothers and I left our town in Uruapan Michoacán to travel north over twenty-four hours by bus to Tijuana, Baja California. Our home-which for the past six years had been where our friends' laughter ran down and up the street, where we played marbles, hide and seek, volleyball, soccer, and where the smell of fresh Mexican bread next door told us it was time for a snack-was now a long distant memory.

My home was now replaced by an evening that began on the hills of San Ysidro, where the meadows and bushes disappeared amid the dark skies, and only a glimpse of light from the Coyote's flashlight guided many families, not just ours, through an unknown route. Here a little seven-year-old girl's imagination substituted reality with a game-like playing hide and seek-in the hills. But what I thought was a hiking adventure soon turned into terror, and the enemy now had a name... "Migra".

In the middle of the journey, the Coyote had decided it was time to rest. We took shelter in a tent made of plastic bags and plastic scraps. Our beds and blankets, too, were made from plastic bags, protecting us from the elements and any unknown hidden dangers.

I was then woken up by an agonizing foot pain, as if knives were repeatedly being daggered into my legs. We had already walked so far that night, that the aching made its way through my skin and penetrated my bones. It felt as if the whole night passed in only a few minutes inside the tent, when suddenly my eldest sister's hand covered my mouth. She heard voices and steps outside looking for us but before they found us, my family and I got out of the tents and started running on what seemed like an impossible mission to save our lives and escape the grasp of the Migra! We were on the longest journey of our lives with only one goal in mind: to stay together and make it across to my father and brother...to reach that American Dream!

Sueños

Ayer, un eterno suspirar
Ahora, un eterno esperar
Mañana, un tal vez o un adiós
¿Dónde fue, cómo fue?
¿Quién puede ser tan cruel?
¿Por qué tú, por qué no yo?
¿Preguntar o reclamar?
Sueños, ¿la esperanza o el dolor?
¿Quién los hace realidad?
¿Quién los hace un llorar?
Quién más puede ser
Sabes o ¿aún quieres preguntar?

Dreams

Yesterday, an eternal why
Today, an eternal sigh
Tomorrow, a could or could not be
Where, how could it be?
Who could be so cruel?
Why you, why not me?
Complain or implore
Dreams, hope or agony?
Who makes them a reality?
Who makes them a despair?
Who else could it be
Do you know, or do you need to plead?

| IRONÍA |

Our life had been far from easy since crossing the San Ysidro border that night. Instead, my family's hard work after crossing the border had little to show for their sacrifice, and sadly, we found ourselves immersed in poverty.

I have a reminder in my head with its own heartbeat telling me that it is true, that the memory of those many times when we did not have a good coat to fight the cold was real. In winter, I walked to elementary school alongside my sister as fast as possible just to get into that four-walled classroom to warm our hands that did not have the comfort of a pair of gloves. There, finally after walking for approximately twenty minutes in the dry winter cold, the warmth would turn our painful red cheeks to a pinkish color and revitalize our bodies' blood flow.

However, school would only last eight hours, and after that, our bodies had to prepare themselves to endure the same thing going back home. Home was not any better, but at least, it sheltered our shivering bodies, maintaining some of the body heat from our family of nine inside the home.

Unfortunately, those winters did not only bring chilly days, but it also meant no agricultural work for my parents, which meant little or no food on the table. Poverty again made its presence felt, but this time with the great reminder from our growling stomachs, letting us know that it was dinner time. A boiling pot of beans on the stove had to suffice as the only source of food for each of our nine stomachs in need of something to eat before going to bed. That dinner along with the heat dissipating from those of us sharing one bedroom would sustain us through the night.

The next day would be a good one, if winter was over or if my parents and older siblings had found work in the orchards pruning trees. However, if that was not the case, we would have a repeat of beans and cold until spring came along and with it, better days that would bring something to eat at home. How far away was the American Dream?

Ironía

Que más se puede pedir
Si no se es totalmente infeliz

Aunque el deseo sea un pecado
La ilusión solo un capricho
El sueño una pesadilla
La locura sea la razón

Del amor se vive embriagado
Las palabras son un dicho
La luna siempre brilla
La familia, una bella invasión

Que más se puede exigir
Si tal vez esto es ser feliz

Aunque, el que pida sea un hincado
Hacia el cielo hay un gran trecho
El pan de hoy es una tortilla
Y la guerra se llama salvación

Irony

What else can one ask for
If one is not entirely unhappy

Even if a wish is an immorality
Hope is just an eccentricity
A dream becomes an anguish
Irrationality is one's sanity

From love, one becomes intoxicated
Words become just a tale
But the moon is always so enlightening
Family, a sign of a beautiful invasion

What else can one demand
Maybe that is contentment

Even if the one asking is kneeling
Heaven is at a great stretch
Instead of water, wine is served
War labels our salvation

| LETRAS CON DESTINO |

During the first few years in Washington state, each day brought new challenges that made us question our place in this strange country that made me feel as if it didn't accept us. We did not know the language, but we also didn't understand the cultural expectations, and without even realizing it, I retreated from society.

Maybe because of this disengagement, I discovered a new method of releasing my anxieties. At least for a few hours it eased the uncertainty of our reality. For a moment, I would be a part of something that understood and accepted me. There it was, a desk, as if it were kneeling in the corner of the bedroom waiting to feel my arms resting against it and releasing the beginning of a revelation. It held on its back a piece of paper and a pencil, whose only hope was to be rescued from their fate and not be thrown into oblivion. It was then when all three elements came together.

My fingers which now held the pencil felt the magnetism pulling it towards the paper on the desk to accomplish their mission and escape. My thoughts came alive and there were no worries of time, space, or reality that could disrupt my concentration. Yes, they were just materials, as insignificant as they might have seemed to others, but for me they gave me a sense of belonging and a place where I did not feel alienated. For many years, they would witness my many feelings I could not express outwardly.

They did not complain about my immature mistakes, they did not distinguish between truth or fantasy. It seemed even as if when I read them back, the words knew me better than I knew myself. Through all the agony and hopelessness, and even those few moments of happiness, I still had that wish, to reach the American Dream!

Letras Con Destino

Un arte que fluye de mi alma
Se apodera de mis manos
Convirtiendo pensamientos y tinta en hermanos
Lo escrito no se olvida
Solo lo inconveniente haces se despida
Después de unas letras, el pecho suspira aire puro
De tus dedos, en un papel escribes un susurro
Ya lograste unas cuantas líneas entendidas
Para descifrar ideas pocas aturdidas
No es que, al mundo, sean debidas
Al contrario, son penas muy dolidas
O fantasías amorosas no pedidas
Hace rato fueron palabras sin destino
Hoy es un tema muy sentido
Pues en un papel has dejado tus suspiros
Esos que quizás un día sean reconocidos
En corazones sean imprimidos

Letters with Destiny

An art that flows through my soul
It takes control over my hands
Thoughts and ink become related
The written cannot be forgotten
Only the inconvenient can be departed
After a few letters, one can exhale
Through my fingers, a sigh has been cemented
A few lines can now be comprehended
Deciphering ideas that are a bit bewildered
It is not that they are owned to the realm
For they are sorrows much lamented
Fantasies not requested
A moment ago, these were words without a destiny
But now it is a thought felt deeply
For in a piece of paper relief is now written
Maybe someday they will be acknowledged
In hearts, possibly become imprinted

| EL CAMPO |

It was the first time I felt like I belonged since that night in those hills. Through a seemingly endless path and years of struggle, the effort was finally paying off. My siblings had finally found their place and achieved what they strived for since our arrival in America-a place to call home. They were all so happy, smiles amid hard work, sleepless nights and forgotten childhoods. Here, at this piece of property on the border of Prosser, just off Highway 12 which still connected us to Grandview and the rest of the Valley, was our new house. My siblings were calling it home and making it as beautiful as possible.

Yes, we had gardens; the fragrance of flowers surrounded our happiness, and we could not help but embrace their beauty through our eyes. The tiresome hours it took them to remove the invasion of weeds and heavy loads of rocks, was not an important inconvenience for they finally had their long-awaited volleyball court just a touch and spike away from our driveway. We even had our own tree which they had brought from work that day. The smiles on their faces showed how excited they were to give this tree life in our new home and how they aspired to witness its growth alongside our new beginning.

A bike ride was all it took during the right season to indulge ourselves with all the raspberries we could eat. We even had neighbors down the street that welcomed us and opened their home for a few of us kids that needed guidance and had much to learn. They taught with their actions that there are people who don't see race but a human being in search of friendship. Could this finally be what it meant to be accepted? Had we made it? Would we finally know what it felt like to be part of the American Dream?

El Campo

En una voz lejana
Pasado renace en presente
Memorias ya guardadas
A la vez, brotan como vida
El olor del campo, no olvido
El cansancio del cuerpo, aun siento
La pisca del alimento
Lamentas y reniegas
Es un esfuerzo no reconocido
Insignificante a los demás
Con un sueño por alcanzar
La pisca del alimento
Orgullo sería renacer
El olor del campo, no olvidar
El cansancio del cuerpo, igual sentir

Fields

A voice whispers in the distance
Past reborn in present
Memories left aside
Suddenly bloom with life
The scent of the fields, I cannot forget
The body's fatigue, I still sigh
The harvest that nourishes
Lamented and renounced
It is a sacrifice not recognized
To others not important
With a dream still yet to be reached
The harvest that nourishes
What a pride to be reborn
The scent of the fields never forgo
The body's exhaustion continue to know

| LANDING STRIP |

Not too long ago, we had to say goodbye to what we knew as our only real home since we migrated to America. Yes, we were technically cheated out of our home by the seller's family claiming a code violation for adding a second trailer house on the land where my uncle and his family lived. The seller also claimed late payments, but their main claim was the code violation. However, the rumors were that the real reason was that the seller's family wanted the land back. So, even though my dad had a way to keep our home by paying the late mortgage and asking my uncle to relocate the second trailer, it seemed he had chosen to take no action. I will probably never know what happened between my dad and my uncle or their conversation, but in my mind, it felt as if he had chosen his brother since we no longer had a home.

It appeared that we were the burden on my dad's shoulders. Could he not have chosen to fight for us? I was a child; however, I felt his actions were wrong and that sentiment traveled its way from my head to my heart. This decision felt as if he had chosen his own family. No, not us...not his children and not his wife.

After that, we had to leave our home behind and we found ourselves surrounded by the walls of an abandoned house, the creaking of the old rotten walls, our shelter. We had to walk outside to an outhouse under less than humane conditions, its structure was holding up for dear life and had no potable water or drainage. And although that shelter was a kind gesture (intended to provide us with a temporary place to live until we got back on our feet) by a kind family who were good friends of our family and to whom I will always be grateful to, it was nonetheless a symbol that we found ourselves in what appeared to be a hell on Earth...where, ironically, the only thing missing was the warmth.

At least we were not completely homeless or seeking shelter at a relative's house for the countless time, like when we first arrived in the US. So, there we were again, under a roof which we needed to call home. And my father, an alcoholic, was so deep in his disease that he could only recognize his own needs. His screams and angry outbursts during his drunken days eclipsed the happy moments we had like when he taught my siblings and me how to make an arrow from dried corn cobs, chicken feathers, and a shaved pointed piece of branch and then we threw them at a hand-painted cardboard target.

My recollection is vague, but it was during our time in this shelter that once again he forgot to protect us. Even though losing our Prosser home was sad, it felt worse when he forgot to renew my siblings' and my immigration applications. Yes, his lack of responsibility could have been his disease, I told myself, for in my mind were some happy times he provided us. Even to this day, I want to believe that his actions were driven by his alcoholism, but the question remained-did he not care? Our home in Prosser was now only a far-away memory, and on top of that, my siblings and my immigration statuses had expired, keeping us even further away from being part of America!

Landing Strip

A plane looking for its landing strip
A train holding tight to its tracks
A car trying to maintain its route on the road
I'm a soul searching for a little hope
I'm the present trying to find its destiny
I'm a DNA strand trying to feel that I belong
Like the world was meant to embrace me
Waking up, I realize it's just my dream
And here I am trapped inside the darkness
That which hides itself in the daylight
A plane which cannot land without its gear
A train which cannot stand without its wheels
A car which cannot proceed without its fuel
I am a lost hope searching for my soul
I am the past ever present
I'm an object lost among a universe

| LAMENTO |

I can still feel his hate that went straight from his eyes into mine and found its way to my soul. Yes, I searched inside of me and found the guts to stand up to my dad and dare him to be a man.

He had started yet another argument with my mother in the living room. When I could no longer ignore the screaming, I stood in his face and told him to back off. I could tell he desperately wanted to slap me. To him, his manhood was being jeopardized. We had such different definitions of what that meant. But I was not going to let it happen. I told myself, he was not going to hit me. Then my nine-year old little brother stood in between my father and me. What courage, he should have just been allowed to be a child, but that had been taken away from him too. In that moment when my father was about to raise his hand, I did not care if it was his alcoholism forcing his hand, or if that was just his excuse the next day. It was not going to happen; I was not going to allow him to transition from verbal to physical abuse. I told him if he ever dared to even lay a hand on us that would be the day he would regret for the rest of his life. Yes, I could feel his hatred but to me it didn't matter if he knew I was done putting up with his verbal abuse. I was the second youngest child, and my older sister and older brother had tried so many times to protect us from his outbursts of rage, but they could only do so much. After all, they were only two and three years older than I was. No, I couldn't do much more either, but at least he knew now we were all protecting each other.

Many times, I could see my siblings' anxiety in their eyes. Their gaze filled with an inability to change things, but they too were only teenagers. They felt so much desperation, and it broke them to be torn between their loving feelings for a father they once knew as kind and responsible, and a distressed father currently in our presence. I, on the other hand, felt hatred. At least I thought it was hatred. I was fourteen, and a teenager only knows black and white. So, if it was not love, it had to be hate, right?

This country, what was it doing to our family? The dream was now a nightmare, we needed to survive day by day!

Lamento

Si en el cielo la luna desvanece
De repente el sol desaparece
Si da miedo al sentir el mundo detenerse
No, no es que el mundo esté a punto de caerse
Ni que el diluvio cerca se encuentre
Es que tu vida se detendrá en medio del silencio
Y es que no vez la salida del vacío
Ese que el desamor te ha mendigado
Sobras del amor que un día fuese a ti brindado
Tu espíritu se sentirá derrotado
El alivio no llegará si no dejas el enfado
Pues como acordarse de quien de la vida está harto
No, no es que la vida haya muerto
Solo que has llegado lejos de los santos
En el abismo más lejano de los astros
Entre las tinieblas más profundas del lamento

Lament

If in the sky the moon dissolves
Suddenly the sun evaporates
If shock is present when feeling like Earth is not rotating
No, it is not that the world is falling into oblivion
Nor that the engulfing flood is upon arrival
It is that your life is at a standstill in the middle of the silence
For you don't see how you can withdraw from the hollow
That which heartbreak has beseeched upon you
Leftovers of the love which in the past was gifted upon you
Your spirit will feel defeated
Relief will not arrive if you don't forgo the frustration
For how can anyone remember whom of life is jaded
No, it is not that life has ended
It is that you are now far from holiness
In the abyss furthest from the universe
Amongst the deepest darkness of lament

| HACIA EL SOL |

"Levántate! Ándale! Es hora de irnos!"

Every morning came the sound of my parents' voices echoing in my dreams...

"Wake up, come on, it's time to go!"

In the distance, a manifestation of another faint, teenage voice, my inner self begging to not wake up, fighting for survival, and telling me that it just wants to sleep one more hour, please, just one more hour. My voice was pleading for mercy, for the day to come as soon as the eyelids let the light in. At four in the morning, I would finally give in to my parents' requests to wake up, like every other morning since spring appeared again.

In this valley made up of cities like Grandview, Prosser, Sunnyside, Toppenish, Zillah and Yakima; the source of livelihoods is the agriculture fields, which from season to season require harvesting by the many immigrant families who have settled around its premises. If we go to work early enough, we are able to help for a few hours and return before school starts. And if we were lucky, we might be on time and not be late to school again. So at four thirty in the morning we would drive from our home in Grandview to the Sunnyside fields. We would drive under the dark skies of the early morning, the car's headlights guiding us, and we'd find ourselves where fields of asparagus were all we could see on both sides.

We'd finally park after about fifteen minutes, and other headlights in the fields let us know we were surrounded by other families who were already working and harvesting the vegetable. We'd get out, open the trunk of the car, strap on our belts, put on our baskets, sharpen our knives, and step into the rows where the crop was ready to be picked.

It was weird to me how when we'd arrive at the fields, although it was dark out, I could see an infinite number of rows of asparagus crops we needed to collect. At least I could watch the sunrise; the sun rays shining against the long spears that bore witness to the sweat, sleepless mornings, and, ironically, shivering bodies, and put a smile of hope on my face. Maybe someday, I would be there, not because I had to be, but because I wanted to be. For a few seconds, I'd stand looking at the sunrise and believe in a better future.

I continued harvesting the crop but at the same time wondered how my older siblings did it throughout their childhoods and teenage years. They had it more difficult than us, working longer hours and more difficult agricultural jobs-they barely even made it to school...my oldest siblings knew hard work at a much younger age than my younger brother and I did.

When it was time to go, reality would hit again. But I guess the early morning routine was not so bad. We only had to endure waking up that early and then going to school for a couple of months before spring turned into summer. Even though there was no school in summer, the cherry orchards would be our next quest. At least then, we would be able to get an extra hour of sleep to dream of all that seemed impossible that day.

Hacia el Sol

Miraste hacia arriba
Miraste hacia el sol
En el horizonte encontraste su amor
Sentiste la gloria en su rayito de luz
En ese momento no había dolor
Tu vida engrandeció
Tu sueño tomó valor
Dándote esperanza, él te agradeció
Miraste hacia arriba
Miraste hacia el sol
En el cielo encontraste su paz
Sentiste la lluvia limpiar tu alma aún más
En ese momento tu mente esclareció
Tu voz se escucho
Tu credo tomo control
Con ilusión, él tu corazón acarició

Towards the Sun

You looked toward the sky
You looked toward the sun
In the horizon, you encountered his love
You felt his glory in his ray of light
In that moment, pain became null
Your life blossomed
Your dream flourished
His appreciation came in the form of faith
You looked toward the sky
You looked toward the sun
In his glory you found his harmony
The rainfall cleansed your soul a bit more
In that moment, your mind found clarity
Your voice was heard
Your beliefs took command
Hope came in a form of a loving caress

| PERDÓN |

I was fifteen years old, and I had a father in front of me who was so different from when I was a six-year-old living in Uruapan Michoacán. I'm not sure why he transitioned from a loving parent into a drunken stranger of a man within the first couple of years of our arrival to the United States. He had so much love to give, but the alcohol took control of his actions and feelings. It seemed like it was a sudden change from one year to the next, as if seeing the morning transition directly into night. This strong man, manipulated by the urge to drink, had been in my life since age seven. To ensure I did not forget the kind, loving parent I once knew, my fifteen-year-old self had to embark on a journey to the past and remember the old version of him.

Yes, going back in time I remember that father. He was the father everyone in our neighborhood in Uruapan envied. He was handsome, elegant, intelligent, strong, loving, and hard working.

When I was about five or so, my dad had just returned from the United States after working most of the year harvesting flowers in Escondido, California. Mom always told us he worked so hard to provide for us and give us a better life, something he couldn't do if he stayed in Mexico. Sometimes my mom would work alongside him for a long stretch of time in California, but this time, she had stayed with us, and we were celebrating his return. We were happy to have him back, embracing us, and even joking around with us.

Our home in Uruapan, which my parents had purchased through so much struggle working long hours, weekends and leaving us behind in Mexico for long periods of time, was filled with laughter and happiness; we were all together again. My siblings were always so proud to show our dad off to all their friends, tell them all how he was the best dad. That was before we migrated to the United States, and later within those four aluminum walls of a beaten down trailer, my fifteen-year-old self could only remember those days. Even though certain memories are hidden beneath the surface, these specific ones are imprinted in my brain, and I fight every waking moment to keep them alive and breathing in my heart. If I don't, it means he never existed, that man who I have not seen in such a long time. The memories remind me that his rage comes from his disease, and this stranger that stands before us is a reflection of how alcohol invaded his mind and body.

How I miss my old father, and now all I can do is embrace those memories in my heart and keep them next to me at night, where a dream will reunite us all one more time.

Perdón

The world is just a fake
It doesn't give, it only takes
It doesn't care about anyone's sake

Y solamente lloro, no una pero varias veces
Es mucho peor al llegar la noche
Cuando la oscuridad ciega los juicios

I have to say goodbye
It doesn't make sense anymore to cry
It wouldn't make a difference if I sigh

Y pienso que fuese diferente si hubiese fe
Quizás las heridas no sangraran
Tal vez no doliera cada vez que tomo aire

We only see the wrong
Perdón por no ver lo demás

My Apologies

The world is just a fake
It doesn't give, it only takes
It doesn't care about anyone's sake

And I cry, not once but several times
It is much worse when nightfall comes
When the darkness blinds all sight

I have to say goodbye
It doesn't make sense anymore to cry
It wouldn't make a difference if I sigh

And I think it could be different if I had faith
Maybe the scars wouldn't bleed
Perhaps my chest wouldn't pull tight when gasping for air

We only see the wrong
My apologies for not seeing beyond

| ¿QUÉ SABE? |

It seemed like a long night-one of those days when a sixth sense tells you something was wrong, and the anxiety makes you restless. Sometimes I think it was just me worrying again about something I had no control over, but then the pit of my stomach ate away at me and took over my own hunger. It would even control my sleep, and my wide-opened eyes would remind me that the darkness was there, and I had no business being awake. However, I could not shut my eyes because my dad was not back yet, and it was pay day.

Since dad was not home yet, I bet he probably used all the money on alcohol. But what if he was jumped by someone while walking back home drunk? Then I wondered if he was okay and prayed to God for his safe return home. I no longer cared about the money that might have been lost as long as he was okay.

Looking back on that day, I didn't realize it then, but later I told myself that maybe God was indeed listening to me that night. I will never know if it was just coincidence, but minutes later I heard the creaking of the old front door which told me he was home.

I still wonder how hard it must be to find faith when you are only fifteen years old and you find yourself praying that your alcoholic father is okay, that he is not drunk, and hasn't lost the rent money for that month. Yet somehow that restless night, I found myself praying to God. Praying was an unexpected action for me since in my younger years, I believed that this God everyone talked about was unreachable to me, that he had, in the transition of my childhood, forgotten about me and my loved ones. I was just a misplaced child. All I could do was dream that one day, God would rescue us from this life, but it seemed like that was only a fantasy.

¿Qué Sabe?

¿Qué sabe el mundo de ti?
Que los pasos son con fin de una meta
Que los llantos, de debilidad, son seña
Que es entonces mejor sonreír para poder fingir

¿Qué sabe la luna de ti?
Que, lloras por conseguir alivio
Que suspiras, por suponer es tu compañía
Que en realidad nada llega si no dejas las fantasías

¿Qué sabe la noche de ti?
Que los anhelos, son tu cobija
Que los sueños son esperanza
Que se esfuman cuando piensas creer los alcanzas

¿Qué sabe la vida de ti?
Que caminas sin saber tu destino
Que crees sin saber las razones
Que se vuelven nada porque solo son ilusiones

Who Knows?

What does the world know about you?
That the steps taken have a purpose in mind
That the tears are but a reminder of your weakness
That it is better to pretend with a smile on your face

What does the moon know about you?
That you cry to find aid
That you sigh thinking it's by your side
That nothing is achieved if you don't forgo your frustrations

What does the night know about you?
That your fantasies are your shield
That your dreams are your hope
That they go up in smoke when you think you have attained them

What does life know about you?
That you walk an unknown route
That you believe without knowing the reasons
That they become obsolete because they are nothing but wishes

| LIFE FORESEES |

I finally graduated high school! I thought this day would never come. Many times I thought about dropping out and leaving the valley, but I could not. I felt like I needed to stay to make sure our little brother was okay, that his future was better than ours. Although we had been a family of six for a while-after we were evicted from our home in Prosser-my two older siblings had moved out three to four years before I graduated. I was the second youngest child, so only them two, my youngest brother, and I knew how bad it had been at home, when all we could do was walk away to avoid the painful tears we'd shed for being so helpless. The three oldest had a better memory of my father since they had moved out of the house to initiate their own paths before my dad's alcoholism reached a chronic stage, prior to us losing our Prosser home, and for that I thank God because it would have broken their hearts to live the agony the four youngest of us did, alongside a selfish and angry human being during his alcoholic rages.

Nonetheless, I stuck around, trying to provide a better life for my little brother for as long as I could. No, I am not saying that every day was painful, but about eighty percent of my life was filled with anger, resentment, and sadness, and the other twenty percent didn't make it out of the storm without its clouds. If I look hard enough, I can see through the clouds and find some happy memories, like when our dad would visit us back in Mexico when we were kids; he would take us out to the city and walk around the plazas, other times he would horseplay and joke around with us, or we would just have small moments when he showed us that he loved us. I hang on to those memories for dear life because I don't want them to get lost in the middle of the uncertainties. It is difficult, nonetheless. I have to dig very deep to find any memory of those days. I had to bury most of my memories to ensure I would be able to forgive and move on...but sometimes I need the good ones to remind myself that even through the darkness there is a glimpse of light that shines.

Now that I had graduated, maybe I would be able to get us to a better place, and the idea of a happy life was not so far-fetched anymore. What seemed impossible was not. After all, I had graduated, I had a job, and we had moved out of that trailer park that housed so many nightmares. It's incredible how just reaching one goal can make a new perspective bloom.

Life Foresees

No...I cannot pretend
Life foresees but it doesn't warn
Just maybe, it wants me to learn

Si en cada paso hay una huella
Y toda experiencia deja un aprendizaje
Puede y sean pistas de la vida
Esas que silenciosamente quiere que observes

No...no te advierte
Pero si anticipa con cada paso inseguro que das
No te garantiza más que solo un quizás
La ironía del querer y del desear

No...no te advierte
Te deja caminar sin ninguna precaución
Dejando al destino girar tu camino
Como una marioneta sin palpito

No es que seas un juguete
Al contrario quiere que un día te atrevas
Que dejes el miedo a un lado
Para poder tomar las riendas de tus metas

No...I cannot pretend
Life foresees but it doesn't warn
Just maybe, it wants me to learn

Life Foresees

No...I cannot pretend
Life foresees but it doesn't warn
Just maybe, it wants me to learn

If every step leaves a footprint
And every experience is a lesson
Maybe these are life's clues
Those that silently want to be perceived

No...it doesn't warn
But it does anticipate every doubtful step
It doesn't guarantee but a possibility
The irony between wishing and a want

No...it doesn't warn
It lets you continue without any caution
Letting destiny guide your path
As a marionette without a heartbeat

It is not that you're a toy
However, it does want you to dare
Leave all fear aside
Take control of all your goals

No...I cannot pretend
Life foresees but it doesn't warn
Just maybe, it wants me to learn

| LA VIDA QUE VIVO |

With tears and desperation, I stood on my knees in the middle of the room asking for a purpose and begging for a why. I had reached my limit and the pain was invading my soul to the point I could feel my heart crushing into pieces. My mind was full of doubts and insecurities that flashed red warnings of "Do Not Enter" to any positive thought. Little compared to that feeling I had that day, as if I didn't know myself or what purpose, if any, I had in this world. I assume we all search for our life's meaning during times of despair. I just didn't realize that I had that life-altering reflection at the age of nineteen. That day I blamed God for abandoning us in a strange place, where I still did not feel like I belonged, in a place that had taught me feelings that no child should ever know.

Growing up, I didn't have the security of a bright future, the security of a warm blanket in the cold winters, the security of a pantry and refrigerator filled with food, or the security of four safe walls that most people called home. No, I had fears and pains that made me grow up too soon to even realize that I was living a life. Yes, I had survived nineteen years, but somehow I did not feel them passing by. The pain at that moment, if possible, increased as I realized that I had only survived, I had not lived. It's ironic how somehow that moment of existence seemed to last forever, and I finally broke. Like shattered glass, my tears ripped through my soul, reminding me that the dream was just that, a dream.

La Vida Que Vivo

The life I have today is the life I never had to live
I made choices and those choices made me who I am
I was at fault but time is to realize that fault is also blame

La vida que vivo hoy es la vida que nunca tuve que vivir
Tome decisiones y esas decisiones me formaron en lo que soy
Pise por donde viví y me hice camino a donde voy
Cuando en mi rostro se figuro dolor tuve que fingir
Me queje sin darme cuenta que me reclamaba yo
Me culpe pero encontré que culpas son compartidas
Escarbe hasta saber que no saldría sola del holló
Fue allí que me llene de luz y sanaron un poco las heridas
El esta allí solo mira y cuenta de darás que Dios es amor
Si hay soledad el sera tu compañía, entonces ya no abra dolor
Recuerda que el día de hoy el te regalo
Para bien o para mal con tus pasos ya tu ruta se marco

The life I have today is the life I never had to live
I made choices and those choices made me who I am
I was at fault but time is to realize that fault is also blame

The Life I Live

The life I have today is the life I never had to live
I made choices and those choices made me who I am
I was a fault but time is to realize that fault is also blame

The life I live today is the life I never had to live
I made choices that made me who I am
I walked a path toward the footprints that are yet to come
I hid the pain when my face felt otherwise
I complained not realizing it was self-reproach
I blamed myself but discovered that faults are also shared
I dug deep and learned that I couldn't pull myself out of the hole
At that moment I saw the light and the healing began
He is there open your eyes and you will see that God is love
In loneliness he will be your guide and no pain will survive
Remember that today is his gift to you
For better or worse your steps created your way

The life I have today is the life I never had to live
I made choices and those choices made me how I am
I was at fault but time is to realize that fault is also blame

| ENFRENA |

I guess it finally happened. I, too, decided it was time to leave and start fresh somewhere else. I felt frustrated looking for a job in the valley, but with no experience in any office setting, it was just too difficult. I was back where I started, working in the fields. I promised myself I would not end up there, not that there's anything wrong with it. I love working outdoors, but it is hard work and yields little pay.

My dreams now seemed so far away with all the financial problems and the same old family drama at home and not being able to go to college since I could not afford it. The only thing that encouraged me was that at least I could help with a little money for bills, rent, and groceries.

My youngest brother had a better place to live now thanks to being part of a housing project. At least he had a better home and his own room. Still, not everything was better. There were still times when our growling stomachs reminded us that we had a fridge that only used up electricity, even though it didn't house what it was meant for. Nonetheless, we managed through those times with the help of our family.

Although I told myself that my youngest brother only had one more year of high school, the despair told me that my future seemed to be running away from me. So, I made a decision, but the pain in my chest was a reminder of what felt like selfishness to leave my little brother behind to live my own life. However, at that same time I could not handle the feeling of helplessness stored in my brain. Once I graduated from high school, I took on a bit more responsibility. Maybe I was influenced by my dad's alcoholism or my need to achieve a better life, and probably like in many other Hispanic families, I, too, took on more of a mature role making decisions for the family. So I decided to move to Southern California, and since my parents sold what few possessions they had, I decided my parents would move there too. My youngest brother would stay with our older brother in order to graduate from the only place he had ever known as home, the city of Grandview. I knew I wouldn't have to worry about him because our older brother had always been there, rain or shine, looking out for us as much as possible.

Throughout it all, our family has been the only certainty we've all had, and that is what has made us strong.

When I finally arrived at what would be my new town in Duarte, California, there was a different vibe, and I wasn't sure if it was the unknown or maybe the hope of a new beginning, but I was there in Southern California searching for a new, hopeful way of life!

Enfrena

Enfrena donde estemos
Ya nos perdimos en esta ciudad tan grande
Donde los automóviles caminan más despacio que la gente
Las casas se hacen una encima de la otra
No hay salida
Menos entrada
Te equivocas en la calle
Esa que tiene, pero no lleva el mismo nombre de la otra
Es aquí donde substituyen bosques con edificios
El árbol que da la sombra se llama palma
Aunque siempre hay una nube nunca llueve
Cuando hay agua se debe a que ya no cabe en los drenajes
Pero siempre hay construcciones tan maravillosas
Enfrena mira a tu lado
Ya nos encontramos en esta ciudad donde da hambre

Stop

Stop where we find ourselves
We are lost in the midst of this unknown city
Where vehicles walk slower than pedestrians
Homes are built one on top of each other
There is no exit
Let alone an entrance
You take a wrong turn
Where it has the same name but it's a different route
It's here where forests are made of buildings
That which we call shade is a palm tree
It doesn't rain yet there is always a cloud above
The water out of the sewers always overflows
Yet the architectural buildings are always outstanding
Stop, look to your side
We find ourselves in a city filled with appetite

| ÉL ESTÁ ALLÍ |

After only less than a year or so after moving to Southern California, dad decided to move back to Grandview, Washington. Then not even a year after his return, he had gone to the doctor because he was feeling sick. When the doctor received the lab test results, my dad was told his diagnosis was far too advanced. Within a matter of days later of him finding out, I was being given the news that shocked me to my core. I knew I cared, but I hadn't realized how much. So much pain had been present between my father and me for so long that I didn't understand the profound love that still existed. I knew we could not change the past, and the future was not ours to decide; we only had the present. Only a few months after receiving the news of his diagnosis, we were suddenly being called by our siblings in Grandview to tell us that it was time to say goodbye to our father.

It seemed unreal since we thought we still had more time with him, and we even had hope that we could win the battle against his cancer disease. At that moment, nothing else mattered but him. Our lives and dreams were placed on hold. My mother, my three brothers, and my older sister had all been there throughout his illness for the past several months and saw that he just didn't want to fight anymore because the pain was invading his soul. Our dad was tired of the chemotherapy treatments which drained all his energy and made him weak.

We knew the inevitable was coming, and we needed to deal with the truth of the situation. Towards the end of his illness, he looked at us as if we were strangers. Yes, a new disease had taken control of him, but this one had no cure. However, at other moments I would catch him smiling at us, his way of saying he knew we were there and everything bad in the past was no longer important. The only thing that mattered in that instant was that we all loved him, and he loved us.

I know that he was no saint and failed as a father, but he was my father, and I loved him dearly (even if I was not a good daughter to him either). Perhaps if I had tried to not be so defensive and bring myself to understand his alcoholism disease better, it would have made a difference. However, I just didn't give him the benefit of the doubt, because to me everything he said and did was influenced by alcohol. I was so used to seeing him in the wrong that I didn't see beyond that. Even on Father's Day I couldn't bring myself to care about celebrating, because to me it was just a holiday we needed to recognize. I could have said thank you every time he made an effort to gather our family together for Sunday meals, but I never did. Maybe I had so much resentment that I just couldn't see beyond the pain of the bad. Nonetheless, today I stand here without resentment, and I know that through thick and thin, our family has always loved each other, and this terrible situation has united us even more. Like I mentioned before, he was not a great father but the legacy he had left behind for us, is each other, and for this inheritance there could never be enough gratitude.

Isabel Valencia

Él Está Allí

Siempre se encuentra allí
Tan seguro como la luz del día
Siempre sencillo, el es así
Transparente como la vista
Cumpliendo su promesa
Él es quien nuestro paso guía
Él es quien nuestro dolor tranquila
Tras un día difícil y pesado
Una sonrisa extraña, nos ha de sanar
Él es nuestro sol a la orilla del mar

He Is There

He is always there
Certain as the day's light
He is always plain
Transparent as our sight
Keeping good to his word
He is the one to lead our way
He is the one to ease the pain
Through a difficult day
A stranger's smile gives us faith
He is our sunset by the ocean's bay

| ENTRE EL TEMBLOR |

It's unreal how time flies by. After a year since losing our dad to cancer, I was finally able to take in this place I had decided to make my new home. With much pain we had to move past the recent tragedy to be able to live our lives. Home was now this new, unfamiliar place which sheltered many uncertainties. It made me feel like an enlightened child discovering a new and wondrous, imaginary life. This small city of Duarte, in Los Angeles County that housed many people, homes, beaches, and forests, seemed to have difficulty keeping up with the pace of its own beating heart. It was so different from back home in Grandview, which although cultivated much agriculture, its endless days were enfolded by its always bleak mood.

I was so taken by the city's presence that at first, I could not see what lay underneath its beauty. The first couple of years, in my almost mid-twenties, I was trying to adjust to the new life I had chosen but how could I do that in a strange place? I welcomed the change with open arms. It took me a few years, but I finally had what I would call a life-how ironic that in my mid-twenties I was finally getting a life with the liberty to have some fun. I guess I must laugh at times to make it humorous instead of pitiful. Nonetheless, there were still many years of sacrifice that passed by and only warned me that there was more of it yet to endure. I was working a full-time desk job which helped pay the bills and where I gained experience and met good friends, but an unknown void in my mind kept announcing itself. It selfishly insisted on discovering the missing ingredient to fill the gap in my soul.

I applied to college believing that was the cry I needed to soothe. At first, I wanted to study psychology but after some internal reasoning about finances, I decided to take on business administration instead. This was a journey that led me to embark on a new challenge. At that moment, I felt the change shoot chills through my spine...after all, sacrifice and dedication make you grow even if it is only out of obligation. I embraced my inner self and ran with it. I had more responsibilities now going to night college, homework, and paying off tuition without any type of financial aid, but with this new challenge I also discovered that I had a need to enjoy life.

This force inside me created a powerful new feeling...I can do it all! I had a full-time job and a newfound admiration for education as a full-time student. It pushed me to achieve my most ambitious goal, which was to make a good living for myself and help my family financially when they needed me.

However, what's life without a little fun? For five years, I maintained a full-time job, full-time school schedule, and full-time celebrating, with no time remaining to worry about evaporating dreams!

Entre El Temblor

Liberarme entre en medio de un temblor
En mi inconsciente busco solo el amor
Encontrar mi hogar en su corazón

Estoy cansada de hospedarme en lo que parece un hotel
Donde la comodidad es disfrazada del placer
Deseo combinar la noche con el amanecer
Despertar estrechada en los brazos de él
A un lado, un café acompañado de un pastel
En mi piel por siempre la dulzura de su miel

Creo enfadarme del tequila saboreado con limón
Que al despertar encuentra la migraña con el sol
Ese que con su rayo me indica camino sin dirección
Mis deseos se estancan como las palabras con licor
Peor aún, se pierden conjunto la razón

Y es que este pensamiento por la ventana echaré
Con el primer trago que me deleite
Dos veces no lo pensaré, mi tendencia es gozar
Y de nuevo mi sensatez entre el temblor he de explorar

In the Midst of an Earthquake

Free myself in the midst of an earthquake
I pursue love within my unconscious
Find my home inside his heart

I'm tired of vacating in what appears to be a resort
Where the luxury masks as happiness
How I wish to turn night into sunrise
Wake up cuddled in his arms
To the smell of fresh coffee and toast
In my skin forever the sweetness of his love

I think I'm over the tequila savored with its lime
In the morning it finds its migraine with the sun
Its rays guide me to a path with no road
My desires get slurred like my words with alcohol
Even worse, they get lost among any logical regard

Still I fear I will throw away this pondering
When I relish that drink yet again
I will not think twice about it for my tendency is to enjoy
And I shall search for sanity amidst an earthquake once again

| PAST IS PRESENT |

I was so busy with work, school, and having fun that love was not on my radar. My childhood taught me that life is pain; so I built a shell to protect myself from what I thought to be the pollution of the outside world. Yet, somehow, I forgot that shells could shatter with a simple crack and expose its contents. So, to protect what was left of my vulnerable spirit, I reinvented a shield made up of a tough and cold exterior. Unfortunately, it did not protect me completely and left my fragile heart vulnerable.

There he was, this man who made me question if I was ready to let love in my heart. I met him one night while having a fun, girl's night out. My friends and I were laughing and having a drink, when he came up to me at the bar. I was immediately in awe of this tall, slender, well-built, and handsome guy who I did not expect to meet that night, but who suddenly had my full attention.

Then, without notice, a few weeks passed by since we met and then started going out, but I had already warned myself to not get attached since I was not ready for such commitment. We kept going out for a few more weeks, and it was all going great. I had even met some of his friends. Then one evening, he began sharing his feelings and hopes for his future. He began describing how he pictured his life partner and how he would be her protector. To be honest, I'm not sure if it was directed at me, but it felt like it when he looked into my eyes. I felt a tremor shoot to my brain and a rush of warmth into my heart. I was feeling an internal hurricane of emotions unbeknownst to him in those minutes. It was in that instance, that my fight or flight instincts triggered me to run.

One second, we were having fun, laughing, and hugging, and the next, I pulled away not only from his embrace but also emotionally. I began to not reply to his texts or calls as often. I would make up excuses to not spend time together, so he eventually gave up, and I guess I broke my own heart. I just didn't realize it at that moment, because, in my mind, I was only protecting myself. He made me feel like I belonged, and that scared me the most. I could not bring myself to understand that I was sabotaging myself. I realize now that deep in my subconscious, I used to think that if I let my guard down and allowed my heart to feel, that he would see that I was a distressed soul that didn't understand where she belonged yet. I like to think I've matured since then and fortunately a stronger version of that woman now stands before me in the mirror.

Past Is Present

I miss you and I can't help it
I try to ignore the feeling
I can't seem to shake it
Our past is always present
Fears that were hiding come to surface
Flashes of our times together I can't fight
Your picture I erase to take you out of sight
Your name still in the back of my mind
The subconscious vivid in my dreams
A tattoo which is permanent for life
Ink that has tainted my veins
Reminder that I still cry our fate
For I have not found acceptance to forsake it
Nor solace to give meaning to our story
But resentment is erasable with therapy
And forgiveness replaces the unheard tears
I miss you and I can't have you
Today reminds me that getting over you is uncertain

| WRITER'S BLOCK |

Here I was, analyzing my life yet again, this time in my thirties. I achieved my goal...I now had a career as a Human Resources Professional and a good life. It seemed at times impossible while I cried, I partied, I drank, and most importantly I laughed a lot. Throughout all of it though, my family remained my number one priority. They were the fuel that kept my mind and body moving. They were the courage that told me, if necessary, I would walk barefoot through sharp rocks to attain my objective. Time flew by, and I can only remember bits and pieces of this period. It's like trying to find that infamous needle in a haystack. However, what lives on in my memory are the most important things: my loved ones and my great career...this was my life. The moments when the family came together during our reunions and we spent countless hours sharing memories, laughter, jokes (even tears and the occasional argument) were all that mattered as long as it was accompanied by the usual Mexican background music, Mexican food, and the love we had for our family.

However, the amnesia I fabricated in my head for all else was a painkiller that aided me in keeping up with my challenges. I felt exhausted trying to grow my career, working endless hours, because it was instilled in me that hard work yields rewards. However, my bank account would have liked to disagree. I was in debt since I had chosen not to take on student loans. I paid for my tuition with cash and credit cards. Not sure how I allowed it, but my irresponsibility of going to the mall and partying was growing the debt.

Perhaps I told myself that spending money and having fun would enable me to carry on without the guilt of the sacrifices being made. It was gravity in a black hole that kept my mind orbiting around the sun. At moments though, I stopped for just one moment to think...maybe I needed time to take a breather and analyze, just some time to doubt the choices I was making. Looking back, I still don't regret anything because I learned from every good thing and every mistake I made. Who would I be without those choices? I like my life and although some of those choices could have been better, they made me not repeat them, and I learned many lessons.

Writer's Block

I want to write my life away
Rewrite the chapters that made me wrong
Live only those that made me kind
Many times I've tried to decide my own fate
There are scripts that overwrite my lines
I hear laughter taunting me
My thoughts are now remorse
Regrets that in the past didn't exist
Mistakes that I believed were meant to teach
I find myself lost alongside my values
Those that I so much used to boast about
Now, just leftovers of what I knew I was
I no longer am able to see where I'm going
Eye contact reminds me of my shame
No strikethroughs, no white outs, no eraser
Never thought I would walk on egg shells
Painful wounds have made me cautious
I walk away before my heart no longer beats
I am a character with no clear plot
Real life story with writer's block

| REALIDAD |

It seemed like the one thing I believed in throughout my life and the path I had to take was him...God. He was the belief system, instilled by my family and my culture, which gave us faith and hope. He was the all-powerful, mighty, loving, and forgiving entity which found residence in my heart. He was this flawless image that someday would come to save us. I got mad at him when I felt abandoned, and I thanked him when I felt protected. I waited patiently for him for over thirty years to show me the way and to shine upon me a bit of glorious light to feel like my life was easier. Perhaps, it was all this waiting and what seemed like an endless struggle, but in my thirties, I began questioning my beliefs and what they meant. I guess my hope's light began to flicker. Or were my beliefs not real and ingrained by my culture as a way to influence my actions? After all, it only seemed logical that if we, as a society, did the right thing then good things would come; however, if we did wrong, then no good should be expected.

I guess there are times when it feels like we might be a piece in a chess game, but when we feel like a pawn in the game, we just need to make the best choice and keep on moving. No, I am no angel...gosh, I'm only a human being, and have made plenty of mistakes and bad judgments which have made me question my actions.

I think about how society has brought us to believe that hard work leads to success and that sacrifices will be recognized. So, those choices that enable us to move forward are made in hopes of a better and less stressful lifestyle. It's hard to understand what is real, but at the end of the day, I had to tell myself that whatever circumstance brought me to my crossroads, the final step is my decision. Through that train of thought, I have learned that it doesn't matter if others might have a say in your destiny, what is important is to believe in yourself, because only one has the power to make the final important decisions of our own lives.

Realidad

El mundo gira, pero estamos estancados
El sol siempre brilla, pero estamos a oscuras
El no escucha los llantos de los niños
El existe, es nuestra esperanza
Le hablamos, ignorando que tal vez no escuche
Le pedimos, sabiendo que puede ser en vano
Todo es cultura que llevamos desde siglos
Todo es creencia preferibles de adoptar
Todo es religión, que nos hace más pecar
Todo es ilusión, que nos hace volver a soñar
Todo es solo idea, de la misma realidad

Reality

The world turns but we are stuck
The sun always shines but we are in the dark
He doesn't hear the children's sobs
He exists, he is our faith
We talk to him, ignoring he might not be there
We pray, knowing it might be in vain
Everything is culture from centuries ago
Everything is beliefs best to obey
Everything is religion made out of immorality
Everything is hope that makes us, a dream yearn
Everything is a theory of the same reality

| SCRAPING THOUGHTS |

My memories are not like a digital slideshow in my head; they appear with my emotions, awakening feelings that I intentionally hid. Suppressing my negative feelings failed to stop me from drowning in my struggles with anxiety. I found myself trying to push down the bad thoughts and fighting with the doubts and choices of my life like water streaming down a channel only to encounter a dam that has stopped its flow.

To be honest, on paper, I was in a good place. I had recently transitioned to a new organization in hopes to grow my career in Human Resources. This opportunity was well-paid and would get me to a better financial place allowing me to begin paying off my debt. However, after a few months in my new role, I realized the lack of challenge it presented was not feeding my mind enough. In addition, it was a long commute and left me a lot of time to ponder my thoughts. After all, I was navigating three freeways-the 210, the 605 and the 405-in that crazy rush hour traffic every weekday. The drive would take up to one hour each way, driving between five to twenty-five miles per hour and suddenly braking to a full stop. It was during those long commutes to and from work that, without fail, my mind would play with my emotions and the uncertainty of what was to come. I would question if I would ever achieve permanent residency or if one day I would just be told I needed to leave the country. If that happened, would I be able to adapt to my old county which I didn't know or have the means to survive financially? Would my hard work pay off and would I climb up the ladder in my career? Would I ever allow myself to open my heart to love and not push it away? That anxiety was so powerful I could feel it overtaking my exterior portrait of a carefree attitude. When would this constant effort to prove that I could make it on my own stop? I asked God or any entity willing to hear me in hopes that a sign would lead me to an answer. But nothing came, and I decided I had enough of this feeling overtaking my mind. So, I decided to replace my anxiety with a more realist attitude. I tried to be my own therapist. Yikes, right? I told myself I had a limited amount of space in my heart for those I loved, and decided my family and friends were the only ones I had room for. I also refocused my direction and set forth more effort into my career, something that was always in the back of my mind to ensure I could help my family and myself live a better financial life and not worry about lack of food like when I was a child. I fought against every pull gravitating towards the negative thoughts trying to enter my mind.

I relieved a lot of that anxiety by surrounding myself with good friends, spending more time with my family, throwing myself at work again and taking on social activities (yes guilty, a lot of partying...but also healthy things like mild exercising and my continued writing). Writing was a great release and sometimes my meditation.

.

Scraping Thoughts

I'm scraping through my thoughts
Digging through my soul
Swimming to the depths of my choices
Flying through the gazing adventurers
Yes, I think I believe I have gone to heaven and hell
Trying to discover the moment I made the wrong turn
Living life as if there was no tomorrow
Realizing that somewhere in the midst of my soul searching
I passed by my destiny
Left behind, a life meant to be plentiful
I'm mapping my steps
Tracing my decisions
Graphing the life that is now a glimpse
Calculating the math that just doesn't seem to sum up
Trying to make way for the footprints that are yet to come

| ES ASÍ |

Do I believe that I'm my own life's navigator? I found myself questioning whether or not I am because I lost my job again.

It was all going great after I switched jobs, and I no longer had the long commute or lack of challenge...until my work permit expired again. This was the second time in a six-year timeframe that it happened but this time I was let go from my job. However, with hopes that my new permit would arrive soon, my employer told me to just keep them updated. Nonetheless, being fired scarred me and took me in a whole new direction that changed my beliefs.

That day is engraved in my mind. I remember because it knocked me off my feet, and I fell into a sense of discomfort. I found myself in a very familiar place, and I needed to wait until someone else decided my future. I questioned the reason I found myself in this situation because I thought I had done everything right and followed every rule the government put in place. I had marked my calendar for the exact day I needed to submit my application so it would be reviewed in a timely manner. However, that didn't work, and my permit expiration date was getting closer. I called every other day to speak to the immigration officers to check on my status. At one point I even went in person to the immigration office in downtown LA to beg them to expedite my case. But that didn't work either. I was a soul without a sense of purpose for over eight months, the amount of time it took the system to process my application. I was able to survive thanks to my retirement savings, which thankfully allowed me to pay my bills and have a little extra to spare.

Coincidently, my sister and her family were about to move to their new home. I was very excited for them and fatefully helping her pack and move enabled me to keep busy for some time. Together, we took down the house's old wallpaper and replaced it with paint. This blessing in disguise prevented my mind from drifting into the unknown negative thoughts for a few weeks.

During this time, I then decided to take a risk. Even though I was without any immigration protection, I planned a few trips to visit my family in other states. It would give me an opportunity to visit my siblings and their families, but I was also hoping to avoid dealing with the anxiety of the situation. I got in my car and hit the road. Phoenix, Arizona; Prescott, Arizona; and Wichita, Kansas were on the list and after that, I would fly to Pasco, Washington.

After a couple months of visiting family, I finally got back home in mid-November. I was hoping to get my permit by then; however, I didn't realize those plans would only fill three of eight months of the wait. It seemed like a prison sentence I needed to fulfill. A sentence that felt easier to carry out because I felt the support of my family throughout the entire time. Every step of the way, they quietly made themselves present to encourage me. I really don't know what I would have done without my family; they are the only certain thing I had since I had little to no control over my immigration status. Yes, that part of my life was up to a stranger and a system that controlled most of my destiny, a system that doesn't acknowledge gray and only sees black and white...no pun intended. This time I'm not referring to race but to a process that will tell me when I can become part of the only home I have known for over twenty-eight years.

Es Así

La vida es así
No explica ni pregunta
Te destruye o te hace
Aunque tengas la razón, te ignora
Si haces mal o haces bien, que importa
Eres uno más de tantos
No hay suficiente tiempo para escucharte
La vida está en ti
Tal vez lejos o a tu alcance
Entre demonios y santos
Es llena o es vacía
Es tuya y sin derechos
Que esperabas, el mundo está repleto
No hay lugar para reconocerte

It Is What It Is

Life is what it is
It doesn't ask or explain itself
It builds you up or alienates you
If you are right, it ignores you
If you are good or bad, it doesn't matter
You are just one amongst the mass
There's no sufficient time to perceive you
Life is in you
Maybe nearby or misplaced
Amongst demons and saints
It is meaningless or abundant
It is yours without exemption
What do you expect? The world is congested
There's no leeway of acceptance

| SOY Y NO SOY |

I was searching through my thoughts... as if I had a question. I guess, in the back of my mind, I'm always waiting for the system to pull the strings and take away the small sense of peace I have regained. Sitting, almost nine months later, in my little one-bedroom apartment in Monrovia, I was staring at my renewed work authorization card, but was worried I might find myself in a similar situation again in a year and five months from now. As I meticulously inspected it, I noticed the renewal date was back dated to November of last year. Even though I was happy that I could start looking for a new job, the expiration date flashed warning signs to my brain. The date was a sign that I could lose a job again in a year and a half. It made me feel like the government could play with my destiny and that it had the power to decide my future.

Don't get me wrong, I'm still a happy, carefree, joking and smiling person that lives life for today and waits to see what happens tomorrow-YOLO. I go out, travel, party, enjoy my time with my family, have the luxury of being at a better financial place when my job is uninterrupted, yet I feel broken. There aren't any physical signs, but I know because the pain inside my soul tells me so. (I guess trying to play my own therapist was a bad idea after all.)

I don't know if it was because it was engraved in me or because I chose to, but I used to believe in religion. Even though I used to question religion occasionally I would still believe it, but losing my job was so impactful that it finally made me lose faith. I still catch myself praising God's name once in a while, but I don't know the reason. Was my heart trying to tell me that I should believe? Maybe saying his name was just a leftover habit from what I was taught in my childhood? Most of my family believes, and their faith remains intact even after their own struggles. I stand there astonished and even amazed, just wondering how that can be possible. After all, they, too, survived a life that had them working as children instead of attending school, going home to a pantry that might not have fed them that day, living with a father that was consumed by his alcoholism, and under an immigration system that didn't recognize them either.

However, maybe they hadn't questioned their faith because they are stronger than I am. So...I guess it's true, I questioned my faith and whether or not I was being misguided by my own judgmental mind. I can only look toward my family in hopes that with their beliefs, there is hope yet for me to find mine again.

Soy Y No Soy

Estoy perdida
Como una sombra que no encuentra la luna
No me conozco
No soy quien ayer tantas veces fui
Y odio no sentir que tengo el control
Y me odio por amarte tanto
Y me odio por no saber dominarme
Y me odio por no conocerme
Y me odio por odiarme
Y estoy aturdida
Al no saber cómo quitarme esta aflicción
Al no entender cuál es la lección por aprender
Al no saber hasta cuando encontraré la salvación
Y soy hipócrita por hacer lo que siempre critiqué
Y soy hipócrita por quererte como si mañana no fuera a venir
Y soy dolor
Ese que no me deja dormir en paz
Ese que me acompaña en el día y al atardecer aún más
Ese que me dice no soy nada ya sin ti
Ese que me cuenta que no soy feliz así
Y soy ajena
A todo lo bueno que ayer siempre miré
A todo lo que siempre supe ser
A toda esa tranquilidad que un día logré
Y me doy cuenta que soy y no soy
Soy lo que nunca quise ser
No soy lo que siempre supe ser
Y no sé cómo encontrarme
Pues por tu culpa en al abismo me perdí
Y ya no sé ni cómo un día, fue que yo sentí

I Am and I am Not

I'm lost
Like a shadow without its moon
I don't know myself
I am not who I used to be
And I hate myself for not feeling in control
And I hate myself for loving you so
And I hate myself for not knowing who I am
And I hate myself for hating myself
And I am confused
For not knowing how to get rid of this affliction
For not understanding the lesson to be learned
For not knowing when salvation will be bestowed
And I am a hypocrite for being what I criticized
And I am a hypocrite for loving you as if there was no tomorrow
And I am pain
That which doesn't give me solace at night
That which accompanies me at day and becomes worst at night
That which tells me I'm nothing without you
That which says I am not happy the way as I am
And I am estranged
To all the good I saw yesterday
To all I knew how to be
To all that tranquility I one day achieved
And I realized who I am and who I am not
I am who I never wanted to be
I am not who I always knew to be
And I don't know how to find myself
Because of you I lost myself in the abyss
And now I don't know how I used to be

| ERA SOLO UN DESLUMBRE |

In my late thirties, I was exhausted trying to understand my purpose in life. I wished I could make the pressure in my chest and the clouds in my head disappear, just like in a movie when one scene transitions to the next.

I had reached what appeared to be a step forward in my path to citizenship; that "American Dream" was just a touch closer now that I had become a permanent resident, but I felt no different than before. Maybe waiting for over thirty years under the Immigration Family Unity Program took a toll on my spirit. Although the program gave me the opportunity to have a work permit and reside in the United States, it did not mean I was part of the county.

When my attorney and I went to my immigration interview, it went well, and I felt confident. As soon as the official interview concluded, we even discussed the LA Dodgers game with the Immigration officer. She was a big fan, and LA had made it to game seven against the Astros. We both had something to aspire to. She, with her hopes of a championship, and me waiting for a positive decision.

A week later, I got an email from my attorney, congratulating me and letting me know my official green card would arrive soon. Yes, I was excited and finally felt a weight being lifted, but somehow it seemed like as soon as I heard the news, my journey to residency was over, and yet I felt no extraordinary change.

So, I questioned myself and wondered if there was an even greater purpose beyond this. Was residency ever the missing piece or did I get lost thinking it was? I keep searching for something that connects the pieces, but I come up empty- handed. So...it must just be me, right?

I decided to take a break from work and the career I had struggled so much to obtain, and I moved away from Monrovia, the city that had become my home, and went to Arizona.

To keep my sanity, I told myself I needed to step away from my current life and get some clarity. Ultimately, I had given up achieving any more career goals and climbing up the ladder in my Human Resources profession. I had transitioned through three organizations in the past four years with no time off in between. I was burnt out from all the hours I was putting in at work. Then my landlord told me that I needed to vacate my apartment so they could bring it up to city code. So, I took it as another sign.

Learning from my previous experience, this time I had put more money in my retirement account. Knowing I was financially good, my choice seemed even easier. I left for Tolleson, Arizona (located west of Phoenix) and spent a year there.

I was now living in a place where I had to drive everywhere instead of being able to walk to my favorite happy hour lounge or bar. However, it was nice being away from the rush of the city. I got to know the Phoenix area by going out to several cool restaurants, bars, and spots.

During this break, I also traveled to other big cities like Atlanta, Las Vegas, and San Antonio for leisure and even made it to Spain. Yet, I think the most transforming thing I did was to take in my thoughts and focus on my writing by visiting local coffee shops, laptop in hand. Meditation helped me realize how ironic it felt becoming a permanent resident, as if it had little effect on me. Now that I had been acknowledged and some of those strings had been abolished...why then did I still feel estranged? I didn't realize it at that moment, but internally I needed to identify and trace the footsteps that had misdirected me all along. My purpose now was to get clarity and learn to live life with a sense of ease and freedom, to just learn to live life with this newfound glory.

Era Solo Un Deslumbre

Quiero perderme
Navegando entre las tormentas que residen en mi cabeza
Las miles de preguntas, que se convirtieron en huracanes
De tanto mareo, revolvieron mis razones
Hoy no sé distinguir entre verdades y ficciones

Quiero desorientarme
Escalando las dudas que asimilan mi fortaleza
Un espejismo que se fue construyendo para del dolor protegerme
Hoy es tan penetrante que no sé cómo tumbarlo
Yo misma me he llegado a creer la alucinación
La altura con la que se suman las indecisiones hoy altera la visión

Quiero extraviarme
Tumbando las puertas que encierran mi conocimiento
Tal vez una de ellas me enseñe mi destino
Detrás de una, ha de habitar mi razón
Esa que se coló entre las incertidumbres
Y no supo reconocer que mi alter ego era solo un deslumbre

"Just an Enchantment"

I want to get distracted
Navigate among the storms residing in my head
The infinite questions transform into hurricanes
All the spiraling mixes up my reasoning
I have lost touch between reality and fiction

I want to get disorientated
Climb over the doubts that mask as strengths
A mirage constructed as a barrier to keep away the pain
It rooted itself so deep that it is not willing to collapse
I found myself believing the barrage of lies
The sum of the indecisions have altered the sight

I want to get absentminded
Overthrow the walls that enclose my judgment
Maybe then I will find my destiny
The other side may contain my serenity
That which crept through the uncertainties
And was unable to see that my alter ego was just an enchantment

| CAN IT BE |

I guess after taking a one-year break and clearing my head, I needed to come back to reality. I told myself that I would only take a year off since, financially, I couldn't go beyond that. So, I began my job search in both Phoenix and Los Angeles and told myself that I would stay or go wherever the opportunity arose. Since I found a job in Los Angeles first, I took it as a sign that my destiny was to return to California. Also, I couldn't keep giving myself the luxury of being without a job. However, that year helped me realize that I would not put my career ahead of my inner peace anymore since that feeling of burn out was not worth it.

I re-entered the working class and returned to California where I would stay with my sister and her family while I found a new rental. Three months later, I found myself settling back in Monrovia once again.

The first couple of months in my studio I reflected on my love life. Looking back, I realized that I purposely pushed the idea of love away, that it was not something I had sacrificed because I was too busy, but that I had turned it away because I was simply scared to be vulnerable. How could I explain the panic I felt at the thought of allowing someone to love me if it just meant that I would eventually be crushed? The anxiety would then trigger a defense mechanism, making me retreat into a shell harder than a rock because I was afraid of being hurt. If I gave into love, all the excuses I made up to avoid it would have been for nothing.

I still struggle trying to understand the demons that lie beneath the surface of my subconscious. It's hard to comprehend how they have power over my emotions to the point that I tell myself that it's for my own good. I have tried digging deep inside to decipher the labyrinth that's buried within my mind and soul, and I end up discovering that the journey I took is another dead end. Why do I not permit myself to break out of my shell?

This fear seems senseless yet so necessary for my survival. At least, that's what I tell myself. So much of my life was dictated by other people, and love felt like allowing someone else to have control over me. I have rebuilt so much of myself throughout the years, and it has been difficult and painful...so yes, I'm afraid. Moving away from Washington to California to find myself helped me gain self-confidence to start fresh in a new place. I challenged myself by having a full-time job and going to college at the same time. Achieving a career as a professional in Human Resources helped me overcome the insecurities of not having a meal or a roof over my head. Learning how to forgive my dad allowed me to break away from resentments that used to fuel my heart with anger and sadness. So, if I fell, how would I stand up again and who would give me the strength? To let someone see me at my weakest, would be the opposite of the image I have created...a strong independent self-sufficient woman.

Can It Be

Is it true, can it be
Walking through the pain
My head is lost in the woods
So beautiful its sight from afar
Yet filled with nightmares and dismay
The many wonders just an illusion
For it hides its treacherous intentions
Deep inside the jungle, a relaxing waterfall
A hike away, reaching out for survival

Is it true, can it be
Running away from the pain
My soul is lost in the seas
So peaceful its sight from afar
Its waters filled with anger and despair
The many silences a captivation
Filled with questions that only seem alluring
For in its core, darkness lives
Deep into the ocean, a relaxing island lies
Is a sail away, drifting far from life

| POST DATA |

With my solitude, thanks to the COVID shutdown, sitting up in my bed, sipping on my cappuccino with the television as background noise, I was thinking about the past. Throughout the years, I ignored the fact that my life had had a destiny that it wanted me to follow. I ignored its pull trying to fight against the decisions that were being established for me.

I've had a not-so-easy path that at times seemed to not be mine, but through it all, I have lived many happy and warm moments. The happy memories with my loved ones outweigh the rest... even that one of ignoring my heart's needs (...or should I say sabotaging myself). I still have much to attain and live for, but most importantly, I need to adjust to a life where the American government has recognized me as a permanent resident. It has finally allowed me, on paper, to be part of the culture-funny since this country is the only one I have known since I arrived as a child.

I can also look back and see that my inner strength came from every challenge I faced and every mistake I made. So many times, I believed that something was directing my life; however, from that came a reaction and a decision I made in consequence. I can see more clearly now how that allowed me to become more centered and resilient. Perhaps it pushed me into embracing myself for exactly who I was. I became responsible, realistic, fun and caring (though, a bit guarded toward love still). And even despite my faults, like my defensiveness, stubbornness and impatience, I was able to tame these in an effort to become a stronger woman.

Post Data

El viento trae un susurro
Es una melodía al ritmo de un latido

Su canción, una letra depresiva
Un vibrado de guitarra diciendo que le extraña
Acompañada de una voz cantando que le adora

Es letra confesando lo que siente a su lado
El imploro, de un secreto no contado
El deseo, de que escuche el recado
El escape del orgullo, ese que prevenía y fuese expresado

Es la caricia de un piano agonizando
Por miedo, de frente no puedo demostrarlo
Escrito en un papel consigue no llorarlo
Finge valentía, con el arte de cantarlo

Es un sentimiento disfrazado en balada
Es una canción divulgando que le ama

Postscript

The wind murmurs a whisper
It's a melody to the rhythm of a heartbeat

Its song, written with distressing stanzas
Strums of a guitar expressing its true blues
Complemented by a voice singing with endearment

Its lyrics confessing what they feel
An urge of a secret not yet told
A wish that the message be heard
An escape from the pride that prevented it from being known

A caress from a piano in agony
Fear prevented it from otherwise being shown
A music sheet blocks the eyes from going teary
Simile of courage, called the art of singing

It's a feeling masked as a ballad
A song disclosing its true love

| ES BONITO |

I thought this day would never come and even though I didn't feel any different when I became a permanent resident, I didn't expect the excitement and rush I felt this time. It had been five years since I gained permanent residency, and this time I had applied to become a US citizen.

When I got my notice for my interview at the Los Angeles immigration office, the emotions raced from my brain and then made pit stops through my heart and gut, provoking an inner sense of stress. Even though months had passed since I had submitted my naturalization application, nothing could prepare me for such a significant moment in life.

September 13, 2023, finally arrived, announcing itself with the ring of my alarm at five in the morning. I did not want to make a big deal about it, so I kept myself tight-lipped about my appointment. I told my family about this very important milestone though, and of course, they shared their congratulations and excitement with me which helped me navigate the uncertainty of the unknown that was to come from this day. I went into the interview thinking that this would be the first step of the process, but unbeknownst to me, after completing my interview and answering several US history and governmental questions, the USCIS officer congratulated me on becoming a US citizen. I was told to head downstairs for the ceremony. I was astonished since I was not expecting such a grand surprise. Let's just say if I had known, jeans would have not been part of my outfit that day.

No, I was not expecting this turn of events so when I was instead directed downstairs where the ceremony would take place that same day, my mind was lost amidst its clouds. My inner thoughts signaled my brain to let the cheer escape and allowed it to exhale from my diaphragm through my lips. However, I had to be proper and suppressed it down to a smile from ear to ear instead.

I walked from the elevator to the reception office. As I waited for my naturalization document, I sat among about fifty other brand-new US citizens waiting for what would be our oath ceremony to begin. Many people sat with me of all other different races: Hispanics, Asians, and Europeans. From their casual outfits, I could decipher that they were not expecting to be sworn in this day either. However, their excitement shined through their smiles and their nervousness trembled through their gestures. They, too, it appeared, wished they had family members with them, to feel their embrace and share in their excitement. We took on that role for one another and encouraged each other with smiles and applause. Yes, we did our best and we turned that immigration office reception area into our auditorium, and our USCIS officer took on the role of the main host on stage. They called upon each one of us to receive our awards as the main stars of the show. The audience, those waiting for their turn, cheered while each one of us embraced the most welcoming acknowledgement from our country!

Es Bonito

Qué bonito es vivir
Sin al miedo tenerle que huir
Sin lo impuro tener que respirar
Encontrar la paz en un reflexionar

Qué bonito es gritar
A través de un lápiz y su palpitar

Qué bonito es sanar
Sin perdones tener que mendigar
Sin excusas que decir
La fe en un rezo descubrir

Qué bonito es vibrar
Al ritmo del viento y su susurrar

Qué bonito es amar
Sin nada en cambio tener que esperar
Sin falsas expectativas que fingir
Poder ver la esperanza en un sonreír

Qué bonito es sentir
En un abrazo, calidez entregar y recibir

Is Beautiful

How beautiful it is to live
Without having from fear to flee
Without having impurities to breathe
Peace in reflection to seek

How beautiful it is to scream
Through a pencil and its beating lead

How beautiful it is to heal
Without having, to for forgiveness, need to beg
Without excuses, having to speak
To discover faith in a plea

How beautiful it is to vibrate
To the rhythm of the wind and its whisper

How beautiful it is to love
Without having to wait for anything in exchange
Without having false expectations to entertain
To be able to see hope in a smile you attain

How beautiful it is to feel
Give and receive warmth in an embrace

| SIMPLEMENTE SOY |

Only a few minutes from Monrovia, in the hills of Sierra Madre, I took nature in through every breath to my inner soul, listening to the stream running down the hill, crashing through rocks to finally find its restful bed. The birds announced tranquility with every chirp. The light of the sun shined through the leaves and branches, caressing them as it fed life into them. Yes, I was now a US citizen in my mid-forties and had a sense of tranquility. Although decades have passed, I'm looking forward to living a life to attain inner peace. I now know that I will allow my destiny to take its course without pushing my own agenda. I will probably never know if I have fulfilled my purpose in life but perhaps, I was looking for assurance in the wrong place since everything points me to knowing that God and my family are that fulfillment.

In a way, this inner tranquility has encouraged me to be open to the possibility of love when it arrives. I'm willing to embrace the possibility of someone showing me that he would like to share in my joys and accompany me in the everyday trials while he holds my hand. Yes, I breathe in hope knowing that I have found hope and a renewed faith. It is like a seed, that with proper levels of nourishment will grow and eventually bloom. I feel closer to God than before and find myself speaking with him and asking for his guidance. It fills my heart and mind with peace and an aspiration for kindness. I look back and yes, there have been many challenges, but the happiness surrounding me is indescribable. My family who I adore, with all my many nieces and nephews, have unknowingly given meaning to my life. Bliss is what we all strive for, but sometimes all it takes is just one walk in nature to remind us that family and their love is joy. Money comes and goes...yes, it definitely helps, but it doesn't guarantee a smile on your face like the laughter surrounding the house filled with one's family.

Maybe after so many years, I finally get it... family and God are what fills one's heart. The rest just allows us to ensure we never take that for granted. However, a cloud surfaces over this tranquility with everyday news forecasting that the current immigration climate entering our atmosphere is man-made, that the sentiment that God fought for has been forgotten and instead of love, hate and ignorance replace the air we inhale. Yes, although I can sit here free, I remind myself that there are plenty of others that still have chains directing their fate and live in fear, and that although there are still many good souls, there are others that forget that with their actions of ignorance they are compromising their own principles. They omit from their beliefs what gives life to this country: the hard work of every immigrant. Who they call an "illegal alien" is actually the backbone that made our country what it is today with such a prosperous economy. Yes, we cultivate it, we build it, we heal it, and we nurture it...enabling others to bear the fruits of their profits without a drop of sweat.

Simplemente Soy

Gracias a las dudas que un día sentí
Gracias a los riesgos que brinque
Gracias a los errores de los que aprendí
Hoy sin pensarlo, simplemente soy

Soy tranquilidad
Que me permite la naturaleza respirar
Que me avisa que sin prisa hay que caminar
Soy calma
Que me regala tiempo de reflexionar
Que me aconseja que creer es mi manual para avanzar
Soy seguridad
Que nació del aprendizaje del ayer
Que me fortalece para mis temores desvanecer
Soy paz
Que alúmina mi amanecer
Que me encamina a un futuro que todavía estar por nacer
Soy fe
Que me sana al orar
Que me regala un poco de la gloria que aspiro a lograr
Soy amor
Que se anuncia en mi hablar
Que me dice que incondicionalmente se debe entregar

Hoy sin pensarlo, simplemente soy
Gracias a las metas que logre
Gracias a las aventuras que compartí
Gracias al amor que sin restricciones recibí

I Simply Am

Thanks to the doubts I once discerned
Thanks to the risks I once engaged
Thanks to the mistakes from which I learned
Today, without thinking, I simply am

I am tranquility
That allows me to gently breathe
That warns me that I must walk without haste
I am serenity
That gives me time to contemplate
That tells me that believing will guide my pace
I am confidence
That arises from yesterday's teachings
That nourishes me with strength, so my fears, I can relinquish
I am peace
That illuminates my dawn
That guides me to a future yet to be drawn
I am faith
That heals me when I pray
That gives hope to the glory I aspire to someday
I am love
That announces itself in my assertion
That tells me I must share it without hesitation

Today, without thinking, I simply am
Thanks to the goals I have achieved
Thanks to the adventures I have shared
Thanks to the unconditional love I have received

ACKNOWLEDGMENTS

I want to thank my family who have always supported me and my decisions, even those stubborn foolish ones, and for accepting me the way I am without judgement, even at my not-so-glamorous moments. Thank you for pushing me to give life to this book and believing in me! Love you all!

Thank you to God for taking care of me even when I didn't realize it. I lost faith for so long, and when I came to you looking for a glimpse of hope, you showed as if you had never left my side. Thank you for protecting and guiding my loved ones and me!

For all the kindness, mischievousness, shared experiences, laughter, excitement, nostalgia, happy hours and even playing hooky from work when it got stressful ...thank you to my friends. I have been fortunate to have encountered kind people in different stages of my life.

Thank you, Davina Ferreira and the Alegria Publishing team, for caring about my project and guiding me through the process of writing my first book with your expertise and knowledge. You and your team have made a dream into something not just real, but tangible.

ABOUT THE WRITER

Isabel Valencia is an author and poet who migrated as a child from Michoacan, Mexico along with her family, to the agricultural area of Yakima Valley Washington. She worked the fields alongside them throughout her youth. She graduated from Grandview High School in 1997, and in 2001 began her journey to Southern California.

Since her move to Los Angeles County, she dedicated her life to achieving a career by going back to college later in life and obtaining her bachelor's degree in 2011. With this milestone, she was able to nurture her career as a Human Resources Professional in hopes of being able to strive for a better life.

Currently residing in the City of Monrovia, Isabel is a daughter, sister to six siblings, sister-in-law, and aunt to twenty-four nieces and nephews. Isabel views her family as her most comforting and significant part of her life. In her free time, she enjoys spending time drinking a cup of coffee in the company of nature, meditation, yoga, reiki, the occasional happy hour with friends, and cultivating her passion of writing poetry.

Migrating to the United States as a seven-year-old child along with her family due to her parents' desires for a better life, Isabel Valencia found herself in a country she called home. In her first collection of poetry and passages, "Postscripts of a Marionette, A-Number in the System", she brings forth reflections of her journey as an immigrant. With this, she finds faith and above all finds the value of family and their unconditional love. She brings forward some anecdotes of her life in hopes that others can see that one has the inner strength to embrace one's path and accept the person one has become.